For Patrick, George and Laura

Other titles by PatrickGeorge:

ISBN 978-0-9562558-1-5
Price: £9.99

ISBN 978-0-9562558-2-2
Price: £6.99

Available from bookstores and online now.
For more information please visit www.patrickgeorge.biz

Copyright © PatrickGeorge 2009

Published in 2009 by
PatrickGeorge
46 Vale Square
Ramsgate
Kent CT11 9DA

ISBN 978-0-9562558-0-8

British Library Cataloguing in Publication Data.
A catalogue record for this book is available from the British Library.

Written, illustrated and designed by PatrickGeorge.
www.patrickgeorge.biz

Printed in England by Willow Print Services on Galerie Silk 170 gsm.
Galerie Silk is a PEFC certified paper.

A drove of bullocks

A compilation of animal group names

PatrickGeorge

A tower of giraffes

The giraffe towers above the rest of us, being the tallest animal in the world. If danger is near, it will break into a 35-mile an hour run and protecting its young, can kill a lion with a kick of its front hooves. Using the giraffe as an early warning system, other grassland animals will graze nearby to feel safe

A business of ferrets
This active sleuth prefers to snoop about at dawn and dusk, sleeping between 14 and 18 hours during the day. Upon waking, it likes to run about and leap in exuberant play before getting down to business. Although it has a short attention span, it can be trained to 'ferret' out rabbits through a system of repetitive rewards.

The Ferret Detectives

www.theferretdetectives.co.uk

A dazzle of zebras

Why zebras have stripes is baffling. No two zebras have identical stripes and it is not clearly apparent why they have them. A dazzling mirage of black and white in the heat of the sun, the zebra could easily confuse its predators, yet it is thought that their unique stripes also help individuals identify one another. Baffled and dazzled we may be – this creature is one of a kind.

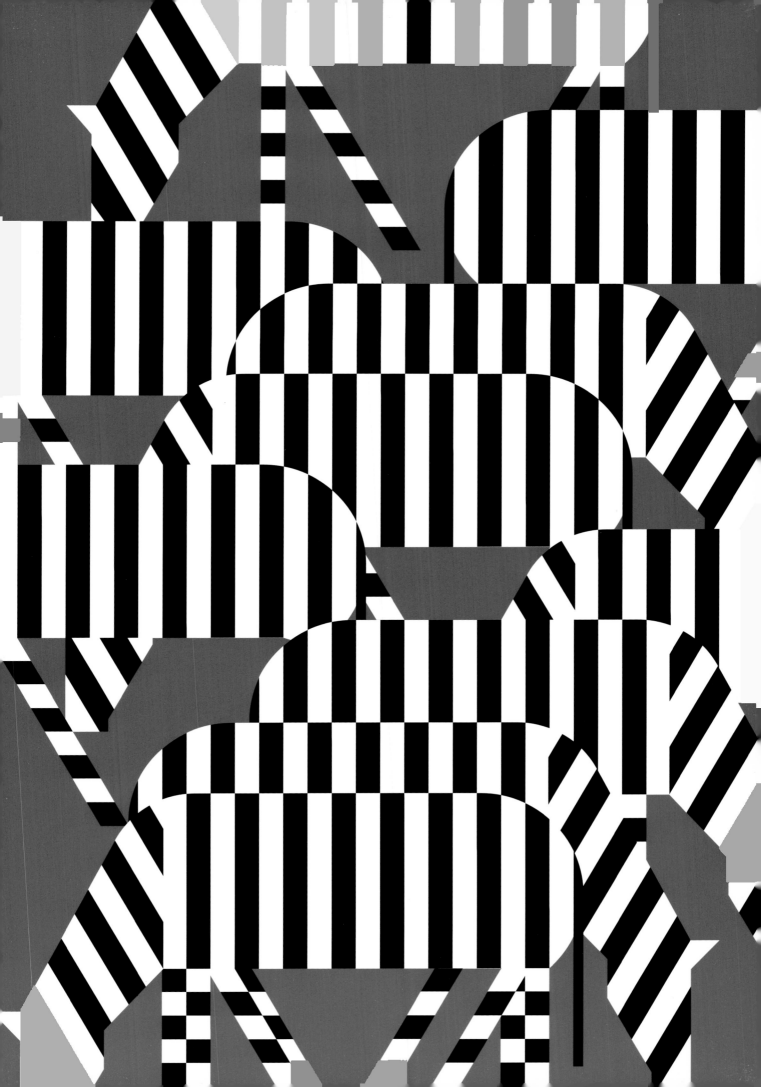

A loveliness of ladybirds
Like the beautiful butterfly, the lovely ladybird
is actually telling its predators how disgusting
it tastes. It secretes an unpleasant substance
to protect itself and its bright colour and spots
serve as a reminder to others to stay away.

A pride of lions
Proud to be the only member of the cat family to live
in a pride and proud to own an impressive mane,
the king of the jungle will laze around during the day.
Regal though it may be, it lets itself down by squabbling
over a kill or stealing food from other animals.

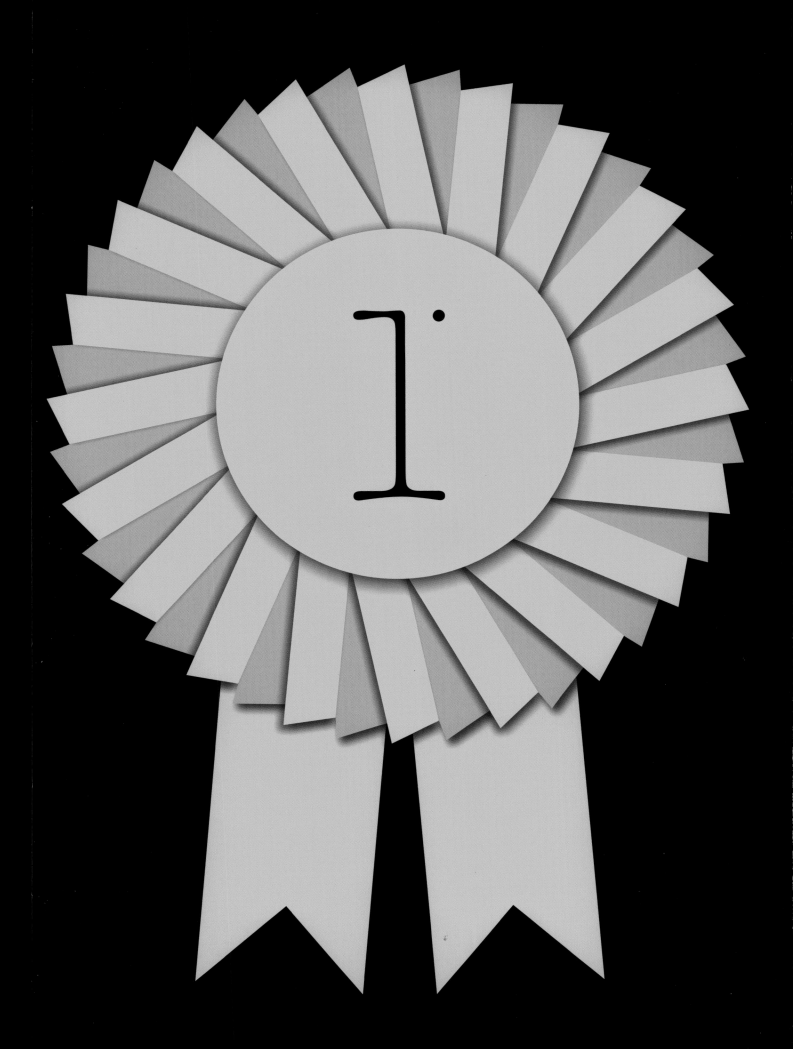

A colony of ants

Leaf cutter ants, bullet ants, trap-jaw ants… the list is endless.
Trap-jaw ants propel themselves into the air using their jaws
to escape predators. Doing it *en masse* they create an effect
of exploding popcorn. They also use their jaws to snap at
their prey 2,300 times faster than the blink of an eye.

An implausibility of gnus
This ungainly animal of awkward appearance is an
implausibly fast runner, able to reach up to 50 miles an
hour in an effort to avoid its many predators. Every year,
it becomes one of nature's finest spectacles – migrating
northwards in herds of up to 1.5 million. An incredible sight!

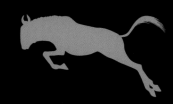

A quiver of cobras

You may quiver when you see a cobra but in fact the cobra is just as likely to recoil when it sees you. A shy reptile that avoids human contact at all costs, it will rear up aggressively and either spit its venom or kill you with a single bite. And you will quiver no more.

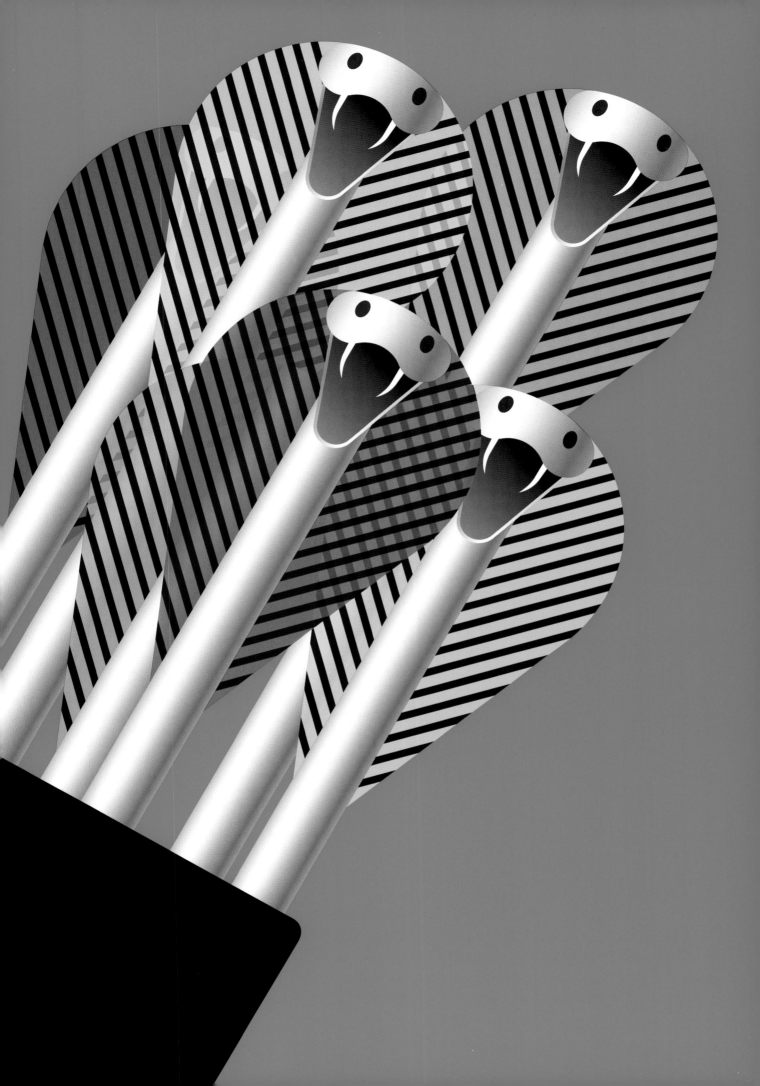

An army of caterpillars
Marching and munching its way through the leaves,
this eating machine prefers to remain unseen, often
working under cover of night, hiding underneath the leaves
so that its cover isn't blown. Some species of young
caterpillar also build a web in which they live, to defend
themselves, before dispersing when nearly fully grown.

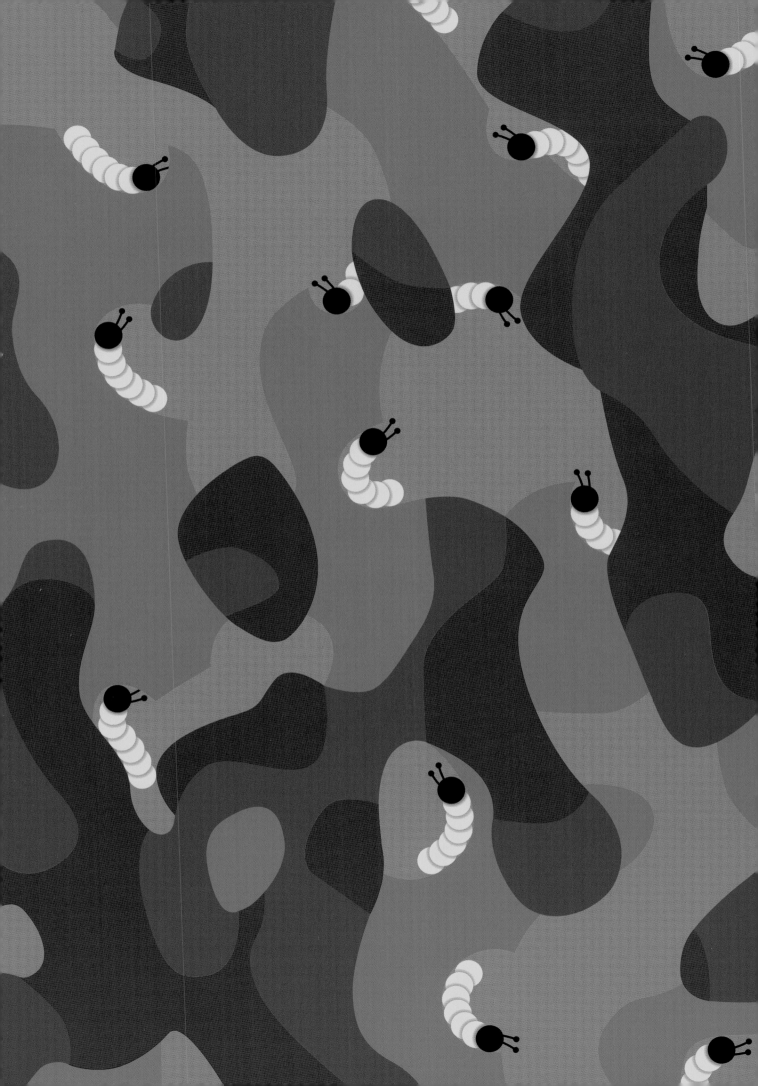

A drove of bullocks
Also known as steers or oxen, they work as a team
pulling and drawing, helping drive transport and
machinery. Often ploughing, hauling, trampling, they
can work twenty at one time or simply in pairs. People
born under the influence of the Ox are kind, logical,
positive, and with their feet firmly planted on the ground.

A kaleidoscope of butterflies
With its kaleidoscopic wings, constantly shifting and
changing, the fragile and vibrantly-coloured butterfly
uses its myriad patterns to good effect. This dainty,
beautiful creature warns predators with its colours that
it is foul-tasting and poisonous. Birds stay well away!

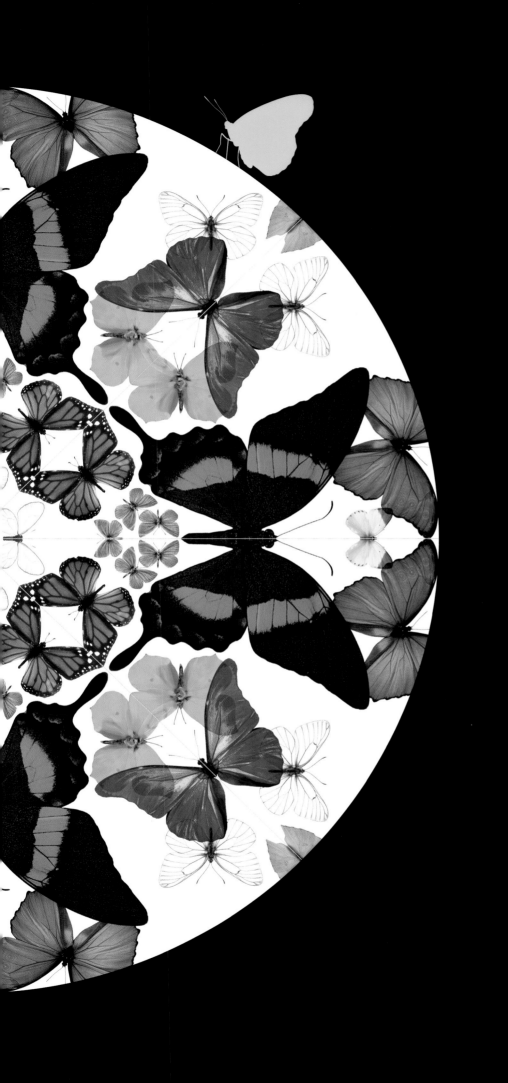

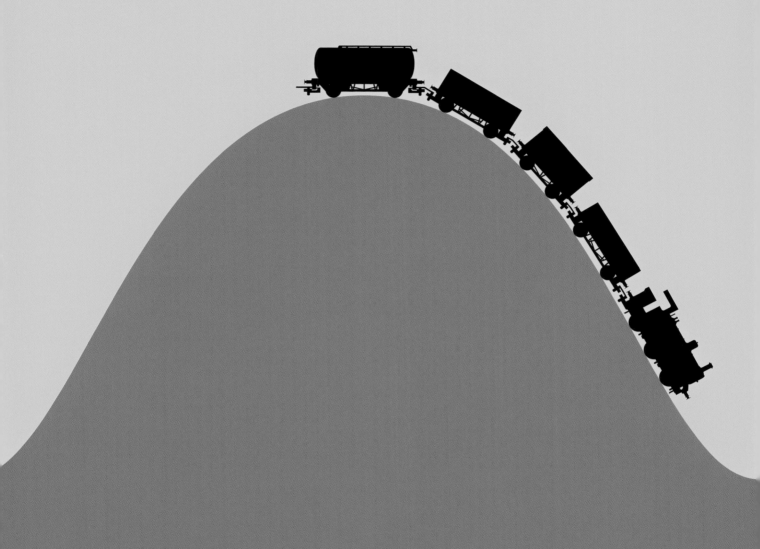

A train of camels
Beasts of burden, these animals have been used in the Sahara for thousands of years. Commonly used for fetching and carrying cargo, the hardy camel train will travel miles a day in seemingly inhospitable conditions. A robust means of transportation, they also provide desert communities with meat, wool, milk and fuel.

A parcel of hogs

The term 'hog' can denote a person who is greedy,
dirty or selfish, yet the pig is intelligent and gentle. With
its keen sense of smell it is used for foraging for truffles,
its skin used for leather and its bristles for brushes.
Add in some pancetta to make a fine parcel of goods!

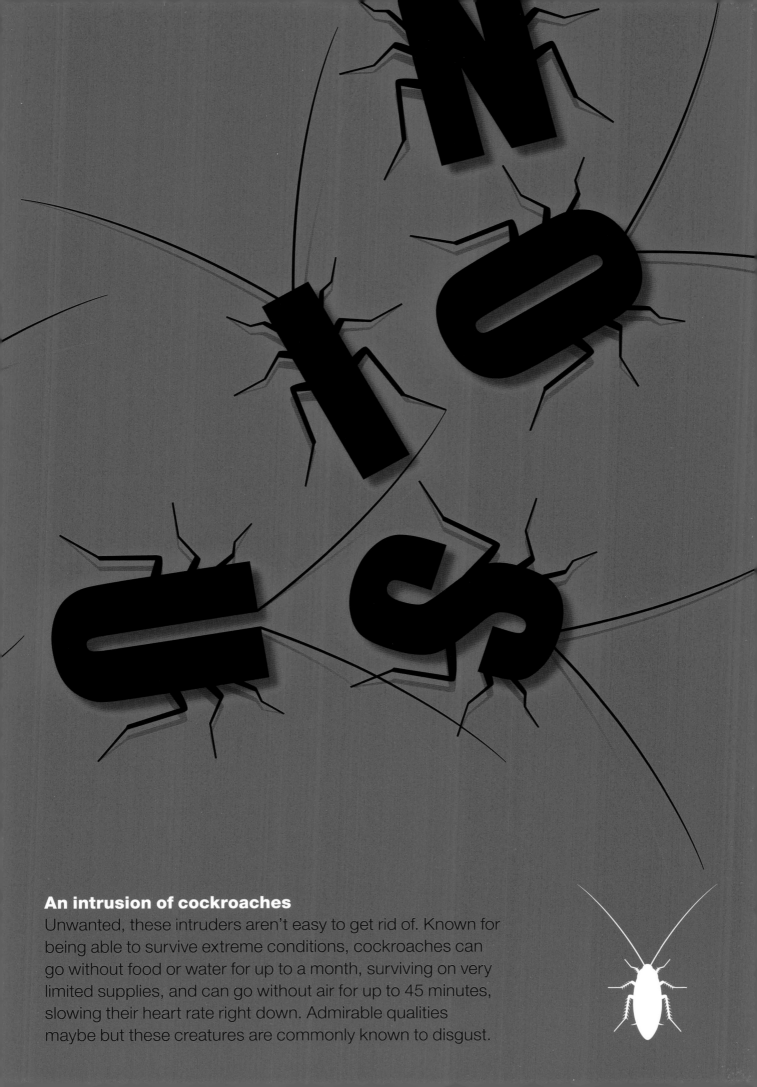

An intrusion of cockroaches

Unwanted, these intruders aren't easy to get rid of. Known for being able to survive extreme conditions, cockroaches can go without food or water for up to a month, surviving on very limited supplies, and can go without air for up to 45 minutes, slowing their heart rate right down. Admirable qualities maybe but these creatures are commonly known to disgust.

A pace of donkeys
The cutely affectionate, patient, persistent donkey
operates at a steady pace, reassuring young foals or
nervous horses and fiercely protecting those it has bonded
with. An intelligent animal with a keen sense of survival,
it will not do anything it deems dangerous but freezes
when threatened as taking flight will get it nowhere.

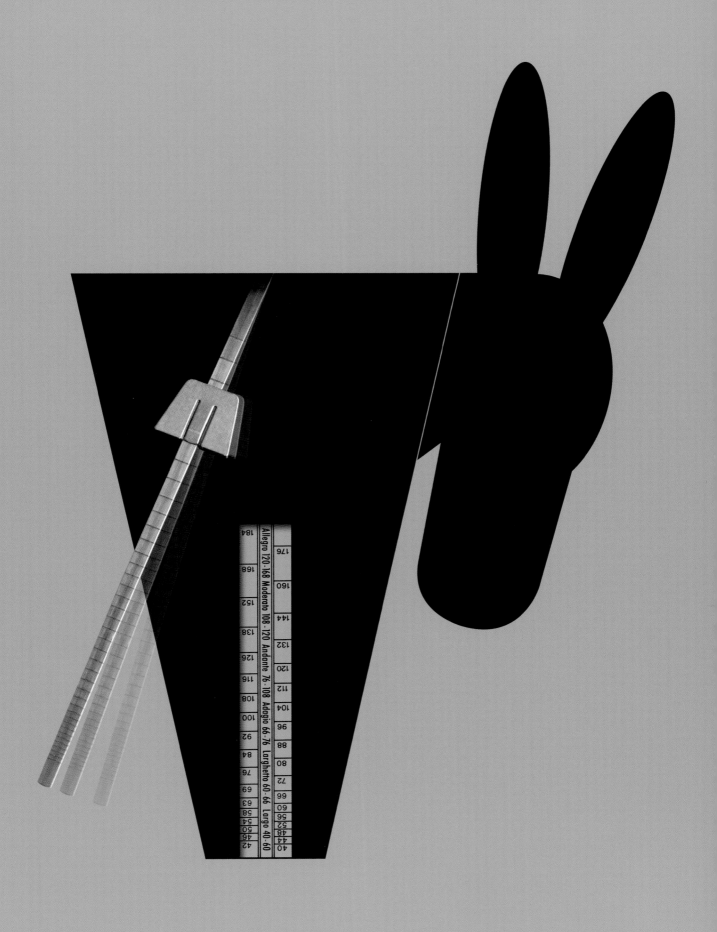

A litter of kittens

Of course, in some countries kittens are treated as litter –
often unwanted and disposed of quite freely. Not many,
however, can resist the appeal of the cute, cuddly kitten
and a kitten in the home will soon adopt you as its surrogate
mother, purring, kneading and trusting. If a cat rolls over
to display its belly, this indicates a feeling of total security.

A hive of bees
The queen bee stays in the hive, laying eggs for a new generation. Her hive of worker bees will visit up to 500 flowers before returning home. And if she dies, another bee will be chosen and fed with royal jelly to make it fertile – and so life goes on.

A trace of rabbits

The ubiquitous rabbit is not difficult to trace. Having been around since Roman times and kept for its meat and fur, this creature has defied disease and is commonly regarded as a pest in many areas. Creating tunnels of up to two metres long, it will scent mark each one with its pellets so that it can trace its way back to the warren.

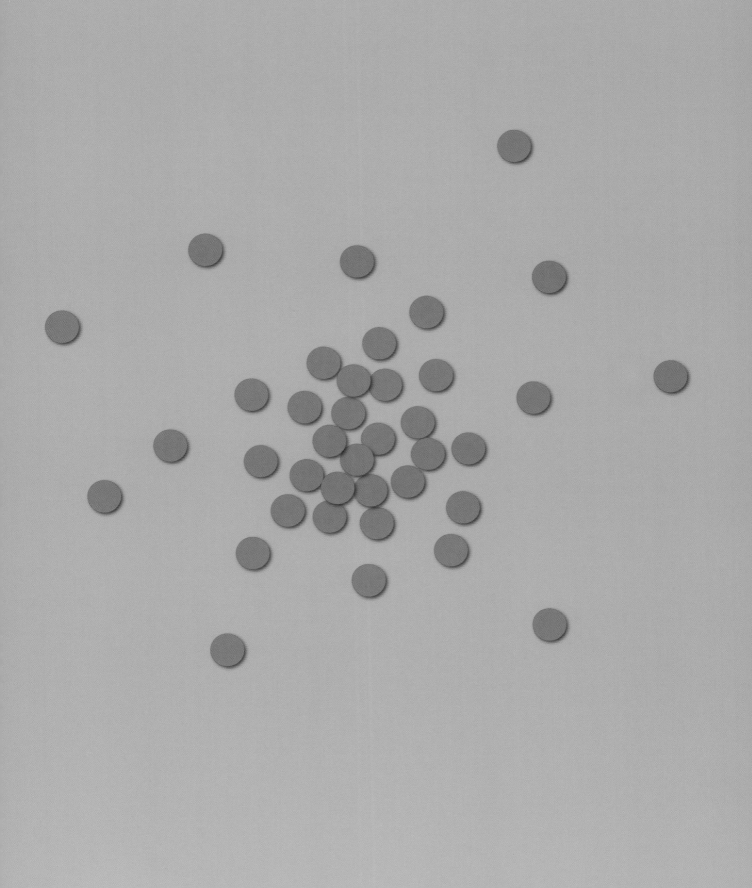

A labour of moles

Tunnelling and burrowing, sometimes at great speed, the mole certainly works hard for a living. Using its enormous spade-like forelimbs, it can create up to 20 metres of new tunnel in a day, trapping insects and worms to eat. It will store any surplus food for leaner times when it can truly appreciate the fruits of its labour.

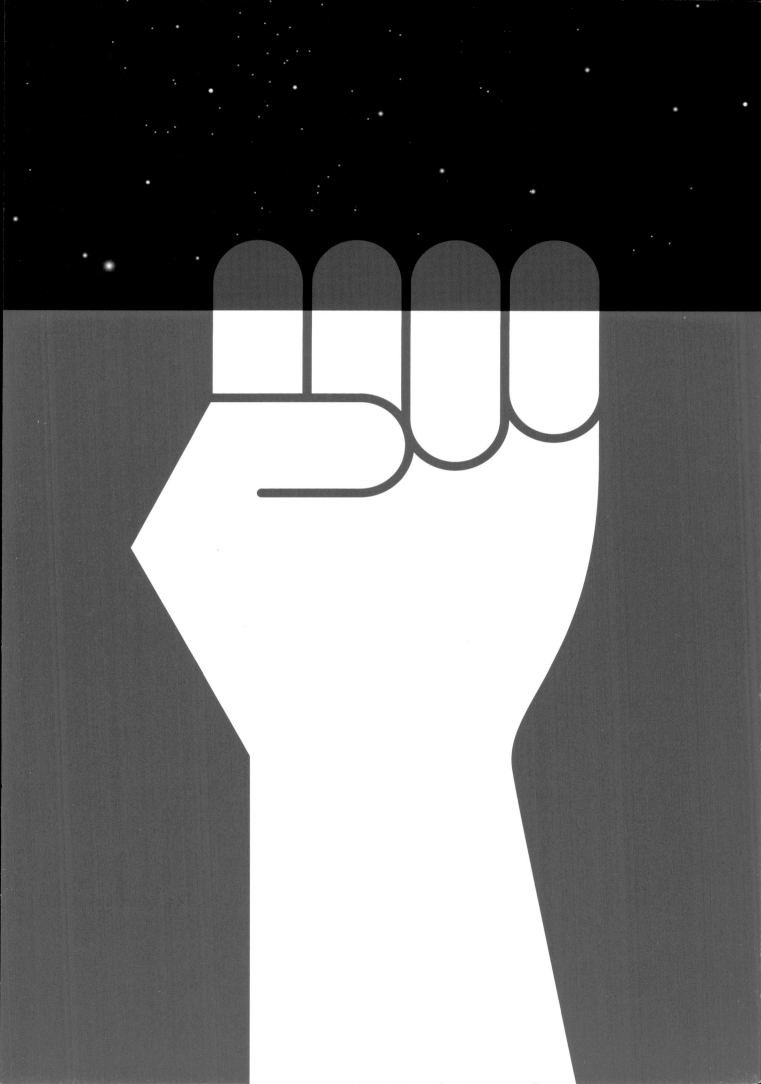

A cloud of bats

Gregarious by nature and living together in their thousands, a black cloud of bats emerge from their roost every evening in search of food. Most rely on echolocation to find insects whilst others use a keen sense of smell and night vision, in search of fruit and flowers.